CURRICULUM FOUNDATION SERIES

SCIENCE STORIES
BOOK TWO

by

WILBUR L. BEAUCHAMP
HARRIET M. FOGG
GERTRUDE CRAMPTON

and

WILLIAM S. GRAY
Reading Director

BASIC STUDIES IN SCIENCE

SCOTT, FORESMAN AND COMPANY
CHICAGO   ATLANTA   DALLAS   NEW YORK

ACKNOWLEDGMENTS

For valuable critical help on *Science Stories, Book Two,* grateful acknowledgment is made to Joe Young West, Professor of Elementary Science, State Teachers College, East Radford, Virginia; Miss Rose Lammel, Assistant Professor of Elementary Science, Colorado State Teachers College; Miss Louise Hearst, Assistant Professor of Teaching, Iowa State Teachers College, Cedar Falls; Miss Eleanor Troxell, Elementary Grade Supervisor, Kalamazoo, Michigan; and others.

Great pains and much expense have been assumed by the publishers of *Science Stories, Book Two,* to provide illustrations which combine child-appeal with scientific validity of form and color.

The combination of these two prime requirements has enlisted the co-operation of the well-known illustrators of children's books, *Miriam Story Hurford, Donn P. Crane,* and *L. Kate Deal,* together with two artists in the scientific field, *Leon L. Pray* of the Field Museum, Chicago, and *Frances Summers Ridgely* of the Illinois State Museum, Springfield.

Acknowledgment is made for copyright permission for photographs secured from the Chicago Aerial Survey Company, and for photographs furnished by United Air Lines, Inc.

PREFACE

Science Stories, Book Two, is the second unit of a group of elementary science books in the Curriculum Foundation Series. Each group of books within the Series provides reading and study experiences in a specific field which parallel and reinforce oral learning activities at the same level.

Science Stories is more than a nature study text. It is organized with regard to fundamental scientific ideas; supplies a content of authentic information; and uses the scientist's method of solving problems by observation and experiment. Thus it provides opportunities for the pupil, even at this early stage, to use scientific information and methods of thinking for better interpreting his environment.

For successful use in the lower grades, science textbooks must recognize the limited reading experience and abilities of children. Unnecessary reading difficulties must be scrupulously avoided. The pupil's effort must be centered upon the study of scientific ideas rather than upon the mere task of reading.

Science Stories, Book Two, has been carefully edited with regard to reading difficulties. The vocabulary is based on that of *Science Stories, Book One,* and of the *Basic Reader, Book One.* But since *Science Stories* is easier than most second readers, it may be successfully undertaken by an average group after any typical first-year reading experience.

3

STORIES

PART THREE—LAND AND WATER

PART FOUR—SUN, MOON, AND STARS

The Sun

The Moon

The Stars

PART FIVE—MAKING WORK EASY

Machines

Electricity

Fire

WEATHER

An Outdoor Party

"Oh, my! Oh, my!" cried Betty. "Today is the day for our party!

"The sun is shining. The sky is blue. It's a fine day for an outdoor party. Hurry, Jim! We must get things ready."

Jim and Betty were busy all morning getting ready for their party.

They helped Mother put tables out in the yard. They carried out table cloths, dishes, and other things for the party.

"There!" said Betty at last. "Everything is ready."

"Not everything," said Mother. "Jim and Betty are not ready. Run and change your clothes before the party begins."

Quickly Betty and Jim got ready.

Soon the boys and girls began to come. When all the children were there, they sat down at the tables.

"This is fun," said Joe. "I would like to eat outdoors every day."

"What if it rained?" asked Sally.

And Tom said, "You would not like to eat outdoors in winter, when it's cold."

"But sometimes we do eat outdoors in winter," said Sally. "We go for walks in winter and take a lunch with us to eat before we start home."

"Oh, yes," said Tom. "But we don't have tables and pretty table cloths like these."

When lunch was almost over, a dark cloud came across the sun. And before the children could eat their cake, a cool wind began to blow. It blew dust into the air, and it blew the table cloths off the tables!

"Oh, dear! Oh, dear!" cried Betty. "It's going to storm!

"Catch the table cloths!

"Take in the tables!"

Everyone helped take things in, and at last they were all inside the house.

The children watched the storm from the windows. They saw the clouds grow bigger and bigger and darker and darker.

There was lightning in the sky, and it began to thunder. Then rain began to splash against the windows.

"The rain storm has stopped our party," said Jim.

"Oh, no," said Mother. "There are some fine indoor games that we can play. We can have our party in the house.

"First, we will eat our cake."

So the children sat around a table and ate their cake. When they were through eating, they had fun playing games.

"The storm did not stop our party after all," said Jim.

Tom laughed. "This started to be an outdoor party," he said. "But now it's an outdoor-indoor party!"

Weather Changes

What kind of weather was it when the children's party began?

What changes were there in the weather while they were eating lunch?

What change was there in the weather after the children went indoors?

Wind changes the weather. A cold wind makes the weather cold, and a cool wind changes a hot day to a cool day. How does a warm wind change the weather?

The wind often blows clouds across the sky. Sometimes it blows dust into the air, and then we have a dust storm.

Rain changes the weather. It changes dry weather to wet weather. Thunder and lightning often come with rain, and then we have thunder storms.

WIND

Air and Wind

Something is moving all about the room!

It is moving in and out through the doors and windows.

You cannot see it.

Do you know what it is? It is air!

Air is everywhere we go. And it is moving all the time.

Sometimes the air moves so slowly that we cannot feel it move. When it moves a little faster, we feel a breeze.

Sometimes we feel the air moving very fast, and then we say the wind is blowing very hard.

The faster the air moves, the harder the wind blows.

What the Wind Moves

The wind blows leaves and papers and dust from place to place.

It pushes against us and often blows our hats into the street. It turns our umbrellas inside out.

Sometimes the wind is so strong that it blows down trees and houses.

Turn back to page 12 and find something else that the wind moves.

Windy weather helps many people.

It helps make the roads and streets dry after a rain. It helps make clothes dry.

It makes windmills work. The wind pushes on the wheel of the windmill and turns the wheel around and around.

As the wheel turns around, it works a pump. It pumps water from a well into the farmer's house. It pumps water for his animals to drink.

15

A Wind Toy

You can make a toy that will turn like a windmill. It is called a pinwheel, and a breeze will make it turn.

Get a square piece of paper and cut it like this.

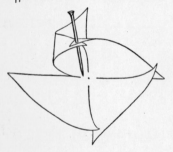

Turn in the corners and run a pin through them, like this.

Push the pin into a long piece of wood. Your pinwheel should look like this.

Things to Find Out

Put your pinwheel outdoors, so that the wind can blow on it.

Does it turn? What makes it turn?

What does the pinwheel do when the wind blows hard? What does it do when there is just a breeze?

What does the pinwheel do when the wind stops blowing?

A pinwheel can show you when the air is moving fast. Watch your pinwheel each day and find out:

1. if the wind blows all the time.

2. if the wind always blows as hard one day as another day.

17

Wind Directions

The wind does not always blow from the same direction. It may blow from the east or from the west or from the north or from the south.

In the first picture the girl is walking toward the south. From what direction is the wind blowing?

The boy is running south. The wind is blowing his hat away. From what direction is it blowing?

How do you know the wind is blowing
in the first picture?

Tell from what direction the wind is
blowing in the first picture.

Tell from what direction the wind is
blowing in the second picture.

An east wind is a wind that blows from
the east. A west wind is a wind that
blows from the west. What is a north
wind? What is a south wind?

The Secret

Jim and Betty were on their way to school.

They walked along by a big wall.

"How warm it is today!" said Betty.

Jim said, "That is because this wall keeps the wind away from us.

"But when we turn the corner, the wind will blow on us. Then it will be cold, for there is a cold east wind blowing."

Betty asked, "How do you know there is an east wind? I don't feel any wind."

Jim just laughed and said, "Oh, that's a secret."

They turned the corner and went east. Then a cold wind blew against them. It blew from the east.

"You are right," said Betty. "There is an east wind blowing."

Next morning Alice walked to school
with Jim and Betty. Before they came
to the corner, Betty said, "It will be very
cold after we turn east."

Jim laughed and said, "No, it is warm
today. The wind is from the south."

"Oh, how do you know?" cried Betty.

"It's a secret," laughed Jim.

That evening Betty was reading a new
book of Jim's. Suddenly she laughed.

"Now I know Jim's secret," she thought.

"A wind vane tells him which way the
wind is blowing."

On the way to school next day Betty watched for a wind vane. On the corner of the wall she saw one.

"There is an east wind today," she said.

Jim looked at Betty and laughed.

"Yes," he said. "But how did you find out about the wind vane?"

"Oh," said Betty, "that's a secret."

The next page shows what Betty read in Jim's book. Does it tell the secret?

The Wind Vane

A wind vane shows the direction of the wind.

The arrow on this wind vane is pointing north. It shows there is a north wind.

An east wind makes the arrow point east.

A west wind makes it point west.

A south wind makes it point south.

The N under the arrow shows which direction is north. S is for south. E is for east. W is for west.

Day	Wind	Sky
Monday	S Warm breeze	Clouds
Tuesday	E Cold, strong wind	Sun
Wednesday	No wind	Rain
Thursday	W	

Keeping a Weather Chart

The children put up a wind vane at school. Then they made a weather chart to tell about the weather every day.

The picture shows part of their chart. Each day they looked at the wind vane to find out which direction the wind was blowing from. What did they put on the chart to show the direction of the wind?

They told how hard the wind blew.

What else did they tell about the wind?

Under "Sky" they put square pieces of colored paper. They used a blue square for a sunny day, a gray square for a cloudy day, and a white square for snow.

What did they use to show rain?

Keep a weather chart in your room.

What will show you if the wind is blowing?

What can a wind vane show?

After you have kept your chart for a few weeks, it will tell you:

1. which winds are often cold where you live.

2. which winds are often warm.

3. if the wind often blows hard.

4. if the wind blows every day.

When you read page 31, you will find out about something else that you can put on your chart.

HEAT FROM THE SUN

Sunshine and Shade

Stand in the sunshine for a little while. Does the sunshine make you feel warm?

Now move into the shade. Are you as warm as you were in the sunshine?

Heat comes to us from the sun.

Anything that is between us and the sun keeps away some of the sun's heat. So we are cooler in the shade than we are in the sunshine.

If we stand in the shade of a tree, the tree is between us and the sun. The tree keeps away some of the sun's heat.

On cloudy days the clouds are between us and the sun. The clouds keep away some of the heat from the sun.

26

Picture 1 shows bright sunshine. It has made the earth and air very warm. It has made the horses warm, too.

Are the horses standing in a good place to cool off? Why?

Picture 2 shows a winter day. The sun has melted some of the snow. Has it melted the snow under the trees? Why?

This picture shows clouds in the sky. But they have not covered the sun.

Do you think the ground is warm where the sunshine touches it?

Will it be cooler when the clouds cover the sun? Why?

Will it be cooler in the evening, after the sun has gone down? Why?

The Thermometer

Jim and Betty had played outdoors all morning. At last Mother called them in for dinner.

"Is it warm outdoors?" she asked.

"Yes," said Jim.

"No," said Betty.

"Well, which is it?" laughed Mother.

"It's warm in the sunshine," said Jim. "It's warmer in the sunshine than it is in the house."

"I think it's warmer in the house," said Betty.

"I know how we can tell," said Mother. She took down a thermometer from the kitchen wall.

"A thermometer tells just how warm the air is," she said.

"It tells us the temperature of the air."

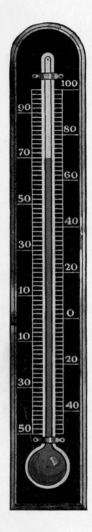

Here is the thermometer that Mother showed the children. Do you see the red line in it?

When the temperature gets warmer, the red line goes up.

When the temperature gets cooler, the line goes down.

Find the top of the red line in the picture. It is at the number 70.

When the children looked at the red line, they saw that the temperature indoors was 70.

Mother took the thermometer outdoors and put it in the sunshine. Soon the red line went up to 80.

Was the temperature warmer outdoors in the sunshine than it was in the house?

Things to Find Out

1. The temperature of your room should be about 68. What is the temperature of your room now?

2. If the temperature outdoors is 80, the weather is very warm.

If the temperature is 50, the air is cool, and you will need a coat.

If the temperature is 30, the air is cold, and you will need a very warm coat.

Put a thermometer in the shade and find out if you need a coat today.

3. Each day find out the temperature and put it on your weather chart.

After a few weeks look at your chart and tell which day was warmest.

What did you write under "Sky" and "Wind" on the warmest day?

Now tell why that day was warmest.

Getting Ready

Each day you get ready for school. You get ready to eat dinner, and you get ready for bed.

Now you must get ready to read the next story in your book.

Here are two things that you must do to get ready. Do them just before you read the next story.

1. Put some water in a teakettle and put it on the stove to heat.

2. Put a pan in the ice box or outdoors where it will get cold.

You will need the teakettle and the cold pan while you are reading the story.

Clouds and Rain

"Father is getting home just in time," said Betty. "There is going to be a thunder storm."

Jim ran to the window and saw his father coming into the yard.

He saw big, dark clouds and lightning in the sky.

Father came running into the kitchen.

"I had to hurry to get here before the storm," he said. "How dark the clouds are! Rain will soon fall from them."

"How does water get into the clouds?" asked Betty.

"Water goes into the air from rivers and lakes, and helps make clouds," said Father. "Water is going into the air all the time, but we can't see it."

"We learned that at school," said Jim.

"We put pans of water outdoors and in the room. The pans got dry because the water went into the air. We put up wet cloths. They got dry, too."

Betty said, "Mother put wet clothes on the line today. Soon they were dry. Did the water go into the air?"

"Yes," said Jim. "Water goes into the air from anything that is wet."

Father said, "There is water going into the air right here in the kitchen.

"Look at the spout of the teakettle."

Over the spout was a small cloud.

"Oh," said Jim. "The water inside the teakettle is boiling and going into the air. It is making a little cloud."

Father said, "The water changes into something else before it makes the cloud. When water goes into the air, it changes into vapor. You can't see vapor.

"Look at that little place between the cloud and the spout of the teakettle. You can't see anything there. But that little place is full of hot vapor. The vapor comes out of the teakettle and changes into a cloud."

"What makes it change into a cloud?" asked Jim.

Father said, "The vapor gets cooler, and so it changes into tiny drops of water. The drops are so light that they can float in the air and make a cloud."

"Is the teakettle cloud like the clouds in the sky?" asked Betty.

"Yes," said Father. "The vapor in the air gets cooler. So it changes to tiny drops of water that float in the air and make clouds in the sky."

Just then came a splash on the window.

"Here come some raindrops from the clouds in the sky," said Betty.

"What big raindrops!" said Jim. "They are much bigger than the drops of water in our teakettle cloud."

"Yes," said Father. "But we can make big drops of water come from our cloud. I'll show you how."

Father got a pan and put it in the ice box until it was very cold. Then he held the pan in the teakettle cloud.

You can find out what came on the pan by doing the same thing with your teakettle and your pan.

First let the water boil until you see a little cloud near the teakettle spout.

Put the cold pan in the cloud. Do not let your hand touch the place that is full of vapor. The vapor is hot and will burn your hand.

What comes on the pan?

What Makes It Rain?

If you did what Father did, you know that big drops of water came on the pan.

The big drops came because the cold pan cooled the tiny drops of water in your teakettle cloud. As the tiny drops got cooler, they ran together and made big drops.

When rain clouds get colder, the tiny drops of water in them run together and make big drops. The big drops are too heavy to float in the air.

So down comes the rain!

And up go our umbrellas!

Wet Weather

Clouds are not always far up in the sky. Sometimes a big cloud is very near the earth, and we call it fog.

Fog floats all around us. Sometimes it looks like thick smoke, and we cannot see through it. But fog is really a cloud like the clouds in the sky.

Fog feels wet. Can you tell why?

We have warm wet weather, and we have cold wet weather.

Sometimes the raindrops turn to ice. Then we have hail or sleet.

In winter the water in the clouds often changes to snow.

Then what good times the boys and girls have!

Do You Know?

1. Does the air ever move so slowly that we cannot feel it move?

2. What is a breeze?

3. What turns the wheel on a windmill and makes the pump work?

4. What does the arrow of a wind vane show? What direction does it point when there is a north wind?

5. What things should you use to keep a weather chart? How do they help?

6. Why is it cooler in the shade than in the sunshine?

7. Which is warmer, a temperature of 70 or a temperature of 80?

8. Why does vapor change into clouds?

9. What makes rain fall from the clouds?

10. What is fog?

11. What are hail and sleet?

LIVING THINGS

Animals in the Woods

Betty and Jim had come with Father and Mother to live in a little house in the woods. They were going to live there all summer.

The first day they had a picnic lunch under the trees. How hungry they were!

But suddenly Betty stopped eating.

"Look!" she said.

Near her was a pretty little animal.

"It's a chipmunk," said Father.

He gave a nut to the chipmunk.

The chipmunk held it in his paws. Quickly he cracked it with his teeth and ate it!

"It is fun to watch him eat!" cried Betty.

"It will be fun to watch other wild animals," said Father. "We can see many rabbits and squirrels and bluejays here."

"Bluejays are not animals, are they?" asked Betty. "They are birds."

"But birds are animals," Father said. "Every living thing is either an animal or a plant. Living things that move about are animals.

"Birds, fish, and insects are animals.

"Trees, grass, and flowers are plants."

"What are insects?" asked Betty.

"Bees, butterflies, grasshoppers, and all kinds of bugs are insects," said Father.

Just then Betty saw that the chipmunk was looking for more food. She gave him some peanuts.

"He can't have all the peanuts today," she said. So after lunch she put the box of peanuts in the house.

Next day the chipmunk came back for food. Betty got the box to give him some more peanuts.

But almost all the peanuts were gone!

"I didn't eat them," said Betty.

"I didn't, either," said Jim.

"I didn't, either," said Mother.

"Well," said Father, "we will watch and see who is taking them."

That night they were sitting quietly near the fire. All at once there was a noise, and peanuts went rolling over the floor. Something had turned the box over!

Then a tiny animal ran across the room.

"It's a mouse!" cried Betty. "It was taking our peanuts!"

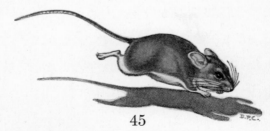

"Maybe it has a nest here," said Father.
Betty and Jim began to look for the nest and soon found it in a big box.

Four queer animal babies were in it. They were soft and pink, and had no fur.

Squeak! Squeak! they went. All they could do was move their feet a little, and open their funny mouths.

"How tiny they are!" cried Betty.

"Food will make them grow," said Mother. "At first their only food is the milk they get from their mother.

"But as they grow larger, they will eat other kinds of food."

46

As the days went by, the baby mice grew fast and soon were covered with fur.

"Now that they have some fur, they are like the mother mouse," said Betty.

"Yes," said Father. "Baby mice grow up to be big mice.

"Baby plants grow up to be big plants.

"And baby boys and girls grow up to be big people.

"All these babies must have food to make them grow. No living thing can live and grow without food."

One day when the children looked in the nest, the young mice were gone!

"They have gone to look for their own food," said Mother.

The mice never came back to the nest.

But sometimes the children would see one of them running across the floor, looking for something to eat.

HOW ANIMALS GET FOOD

Do Animals Need Food?

Could we live and grow without food?

How do we put food into our mouths?

Do our pets need food?

What do cats and dogs eat?

Why do they need sharp teeth?

How do they get milk into their mouths?

What other animals have you seen eating?

What food did they eat?

How did they get their food?

Animals use other living things for food. Some animals eat plants, and some eat other animals. And some eat both plants and animals.

Do you eat both plants and animals?

48

Large Animals

A horse eats grass and other plants. It is easy for him to get food. He just puts his head down and eats the plants from the ground. His sharp teeth cut them off.

Look at the picture of the horse and tell how his neck helps him get grass.

An elephant eats plants, too.

Look at his long trunk and see how he picks the plants that he eats.

The elephant's neck is so short that he cannot put his head down to eat. So he picks up his food with his trunk and lifts it up to his mouth. His trunk is really a very long nose. Think of putting your food into your mouth with your nose!

Bears eat parts of plants. They eat fruit, corn, roots, and nuts.

But plants are not the only food that bears eat. They eat many animals. They eat almost any animal they can catch.

 A bear has very sharp, strong claws that help him catch other animals. His claws help him dig up roots. They make it easy for him to climb trees to get honey from the nests of bees.

Bears can catch fish. What part of his body does a bear use to catch fish?

Nanook, the White Bear

Nanook was a big white bear. He lived far up in the north, where there is much ice and snow. But his thick white fur kept him warm.

On Nanook's big feet were strong, sharp claws. Nanook had sharp teeth, too. He used his claws and teeth to catch fish and seals.

Nanook was very strong. His jaws and neck were so strong that he could lift a big seal out of the water on to the ice.

The only animal that Nanook was afraid of was a big walrus. A big walrus has very long, sharp tusks, and Nanook was afraid of the tusks.

Nanook had a good way to catch seals. He would stay quietly on the ice near the water and wait for a seal to swim by.

When a seal came along, Nanook would strike it with one of his strong front paws. Then he would pick it up in his jaws and lift it out of the water.

One morning Nanook was waiting near the water to catch a seal.

At last he saw something swimming toward him.

He waited very quietly on the ice until it came near. Then he lifted his paw to strike it.

But it was not a seal. It was a big walrus! And it had sharp tusks!

The big walrus looked at Nanook, and Nanook looked at the walrus and his long, sharp tusks.

Nanook began to back slowly away. He watched the walrus, and the big walrus watched him.

Then Nanook turned and ran as fast as he could across the ice.

He did not try to catch a seal again that day. After a while he caught some fish and ate them.

But how he would have liked a seal!

Coyote

Raccoon

Small Animals

The coyote eats rabbits, chipmunks, chickens, and other little animals. He has to run very fast to catch them.

He has big jaws and sharp teeth.

Coyotes have soft pads on their feet, and so they move very quietly. How do pads on their feet help coyotes get food?

The raccoon eats parts of plants, and he eats animals, too.

He has padded feet, and sharp claws and teeth. How do they help him get food?

54

The raccoon's paws are much like hands. They can take hold of things just as people's hands do.

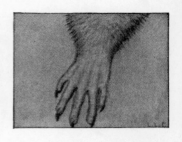

The raccoon uses his paws to pull ears of corn from corn plants. He uses them to catch birds and frogs and chickens.

What is this animal? It eats many mice. Its big mouth and sharp teeth help it catch and hold its food.

Fish eat insects, worms, smaller fish, and other food.

This fish has a big mouth and sharp teeth. How do they help the fish get food?

55

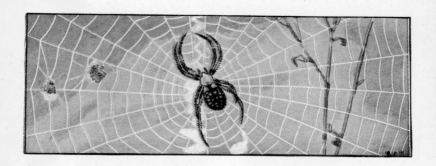

A garden spider eats many kinds of insects. But it does not hunt for them as some animals hunt for food.

The spider makes a web which catches insects that are flying in the air. The picture at the top of the page shows a garden spider and its web.

A grasshopper eats plants. It has very sharp jaws that cut into the leaves.

The ant uses its jaws to pick up food.

56

Swallow

Flicker

The swallow eats insects. He can fly very fast and can turn in the air quickly. So he can catch insects that fly.

What parts of his body does the swallow use to catch insects?

The flicker eats insects, too. He uses his bill to dig up ant hills and to pick insects out of tree trunks.

Why is the flicker's bill a good one for getting his food?

The bird in Picture 1 says "Bob-white! Bob-white!" So he is called Bob-white.

He uses his short, strong bill to crack seeds. He eats many weed seeds.

What bird is in the second picture?

He looks for food at night. His eyes see well at night, and so he can catch mice and other little animals.

What else helps him get food?

What Birds Do You Know?

Look at the bird pictures on page 57.
What color is a swallow's head?
What color are its back and wings?
What color is its breast?
What color is its throat?
What color is its tail?
What kind of bill does a swallow have?

What bird is in the second picture on page 57? What birds are on page 58?
Look at each bird and tell:
1. the color of the parts of its body.
2. what kind of bill it has.
3. what it eats.

Name another bird that you know, and tell how it gets food. Tell what it eats.
Watch for other birds. Find out what they eat and how they get their food.

Baby Animals

Do baby animals need food? Why?

Some baby animals can get their own food, even when they are very young. When baby chickens are only a few days old, they can run about with their mother and hunt for food.

But many baby animals cannot hunt for their own food. How do they get it?

Name some baby animals that get milk from their mothers.

Name some animals that carry food to their babies.

What do young robins eat?

What do young flickers eat?

Can they get their own food when they are tiny babies? Why?

Do they learn to get their food when they grow bigger?

The first picture shows two young bears looking for bugs and worms to eat.

When the bears were very tiny, they took milk from their mother. Now they are big enough to eat the same kind of food the mother bear eats.

What are the young raccoons doing?

Have they learned to get their own food?

What must all baby animals learn to do as they grow larger?

Food in Winter

All summer the gardens, woods, and fields are full of animals hunting for food.

We see bees and ants and spiders and birds. We see chipmunks and raccoons and skunks and many other animals.

Do we see all these animals in winter?

Many animals make warm homes and do not come out in cold weather.

But they must have food.

Some of them store up food in their homes before the cold weather comes. Then they have food to eat in winter.

Chipmunks and squirrels store up nuts.

In summer bees get food from flowers. They make honey and store it. Ants carry crumbs and other food into their nests.

Could bees and ants get food in winter if they did not store it? Why?

Skunk

Some animals make warm homes and sleep all winter. They eat so much food before winter comes that they grow very fat. This fat keeps them alive while they are taking their long winter sleep.

Bears get very fat in the summer and fall. Then they sleep through the winter. The skunk sleeps in the coldest weather but goes out to hunt for food when it is not so cold. He catches mice and other little animals, and digs up insects.

Deer

The deer looks for food all winter. He eats twigs and old grass and other small plants. When snow covers the ground, the deer pushes the snow away with his nose or with his front feet.

The coyote and the rabbit hunt for food in winter, too. So do the fox, the wolf, and a great many other animals.

The Tree That Bloomed in Winter

All night long the snow had fallen. When Jim and Betty came to breakfast, snow covered everything in the back yard.

Mother said, "It will be hard for the birds to find food after this snow."

"What birds?" asked Jim. "I thought the birds had gone south for the winter."

"Many birds have gone south," said Mother. "But some birds stay here all winter. Some birds live farther north in summer and come here for the winter."

"What do they eat?" asked Jim.

"Almost any kind of food they can find," said Mother.

"They eat the seeds of dry plants in the fields and woods and gardens. When snow covers the ground, many people put out seeds and other food for the birds."

"I wish we had some seeds to give the birds," said Betty.

"We will give them sunflower seeds," said Mother. "They will crack the seeds with their bills and eat the inside. And here is another kind of seed for them."

Mother took something out of a can and put it into the corn popper.

"Pop corn!" cried Jim. "We are going to pop some corn for the birds!"

"The birds won't have to crack the pop corn," said Betty. "We crack it for them when we pop it!"

The children popped the corn and put it on strings. Jim cut apples into pieces.

"We will give the birds some bread crumbs, too," Mother said.

"And we will put out some acorns for the squirrels, and a pan of water. It is hard for animals to get water in winter."

66

When everything was ready, Jim and Betty pushed the snow away from under a little tree in the back yard.

They put the sunflower seeds and bread crumbs and acorns on the ground. They put the strings of popcorn and pieces of apple on the tree.

"Oh, my!" cried Betty. "How pretty it is."

"Yes," said Jim. "The tree looks as if it were in bloom!"

They went indoors and watched the tree. Soon Jim said, "I see two chickadees. They are the small birds with black on their heads and throats."

"I see a bluejay!" cried Betty. "Will he frighten the chickadees away?"

Mother said, "No, the chickadees are not afraid of him."

"There is a red-headed woodpecker!" cried Jim. "He is picking up an acorn.

"Oh, there he goes!"

The woodpecker flew straight to the trunk of an old oak tree.

"He took the acorn along," said Betty. "But what is he doing with it now?"

Mother laughed.

"He is cracking it," she said.

"He pushes the acorn into a crack in the tree trunk.

"Next he strikes at it with his bill until he opens it. Then he eats the nut inside."

"What a funny nut-cracker he is!" laughed Betty.

"He uses the tree trunk as a place to store food, too," said Mother.

"He stores away acorns and other nuts by pushing them into cracks in the tree trunk. Then he has nuts to eat when other food is hard to find."

As the days went by, many birds came to the little tree. Bluejays came, and many, many chickadees. The woodpecker came every day for acorns.

Squirrels often came to the tree. One morning Jim put some peanuts under the tree. How the squirrels liked them! The woodpecker ate them, too.

Every day Betty and Jim put water in the pan under the tree. All winter long they kept the little tree full of good things for the birds.

And all winter long the birds came to their tree that bloomed in winter.

Do You Know?

1. Which of these are living things?

table	insect	pump	sleet
plant	smoke	windmill	animal
stove	bird	paper	wagon

2. Which of these are animals, and which are plants?

lettuce	tree	fly	spider
chickadee	deer	grass	skunk
woodpecker	bee	carrot	flicker

3. How can you tell one kind of bird from another kind?

4. Do animals grow? What must they have to make them grow?

5. Do all animals get food in the same way? Name four animals. Tell what each one eats and how it gets its food.

6. What must every baby animal learn?

HOW PLANTS GET FOOD

Getting Ready

Can living things grow without food?

Are plants alive? Do they grow? Do they need food to make them grow?

Plants can't move from place to place to get food, as animals do. They get their food in a very different way.

The story on page 74 tells how plants get food. Before you read it, ask your teacher to help you do these two things:

1. Put some red coloring in a glass of water. Pull up a small growing plant and wash the soil from the roots. Put the plant in the glass, and leave it in the shade for a day.

2. Plant some grass seeds in two pots of garden soil. Put them in a dark, warm place, and give them water each day.

Page 77 tells you something about a potato. Get ready to find out what it is.

Run pins into a piece of potato and put it over a glass of water.

Put the glass in a warm, dark place. Keep enough water in the glass so that the potato touches the water.

The story on page 80 will tell you about the seeds of plants. You can learn more about seeds if you get ready now.

1. Plant some beans in a window box.

2. Plant a few beans in a glass of soil, so that they are against the sides of the glass. Put the glass in the window.

Water the beans a little each day.

Making Food

What would you think if you should sit down for dinner and find on the table just these two things:

A glass of water

A glass of air

What if Mother should say, "That is all there is to eat. So put the air and water together and make your food."

You would soon be very, very hungry, for you cannot do that. No one else can.

But every green plant can do it!

The leaves of the plant make most of its food. To make food, the leaves need:

Water
Air
Sunlight

Plants get water from the soil. Water soaks into the roots and goes up into the stems and leaves.

Look at the plant that you put into the glass of red water.

Look for little red lines that run along the roots and up into the stem and leaves.

These lines show where the red water has gone up into the veins of the leaves.

The water from the soil goes into a plant in just the same way. It soaks into the roots. Then it goes up the stem of the plant into the leaves.

Air goes into the leaves, too. It goes through tiny holes in the blades of the leaves. The holes are so small that you cannot see them.

No one knows how a plant makes food from air and water. That is one of the biggest secrets in the world!

We know part of the secret. We know that only green plants make food. And they cannot make food without sunlight.

Look at the grass that you are growing in the dark. Can it make food? Why?

Put both pots in the sunlight. In a day or two the light will make the plants turn green. Then they can make food.

After they have turned green, put one pot back in the dark.

Find out which will live longer, the plants that have sunlight or the plants that do not have sunlight.

Storing Food

The picture shows the stems and leaves of new plants growing from an old potato.

Can these new plants make food? Why?

Look at the piece of potato that you put in the dark. Are stems of new plants growing from it?

Can the new plants make food? Why?

These new plants had to have food to grow. But they did not make their own food. They used food from the potato.

The potato was once part of a large plant growing in the ground. The large plant could make food. Its roots could take water from the soil, and its leaves had air and sunlight.

The large plant did not use all its food in growing. It stored away some food in  stems that grew under the ground. These underground stems were new potatoes.

The plant stored more and more food, and the new potatoes grew bigger. They were full of food that young plants could use when they began to grow!

Plants store away food in their roots and stems, and in their seeds.

 The carrots and beets that we eat are big roots. In them is food which the plants have stored.

There is stored food in flower bulbs and onion bulbs. Find out if young plants grow from bulbs.

Inside every seed is some food that the plant has stored away.

There is something else in the seed, too.

Cut a bean seed open and look for a baby plant inside it.

The baby plant has a root and two tiny leaves. The hard, yellow part of the seed is the food that is stored away.

When the baby plant begins to grow, it uses the stored food. This food keeps it growing until it is large enough to make its own food.

Every seed has a baby plant inside it. Some seeds are very tiny, but inside each one is a baby plant. And all around the baby plant there is food that it uses when it begins to grow.

Did your grass plants grow before they could make food? Why?

How Betty Kept the Seeds

One spring day Mother and Betty were planting seeds in the flower garden.

They planted pansies and nasturtiums. By the high garden wall they planted sunflowers.

Then Mother opened a box and showed Betty some big red and brown seeds.

"Oh, these are pretty seeds!" cried Betty.

"They look like beans, but the white beans we eat are not as pretty as these.

"What kind of seeds are they?"

"They are the seeds of the scarlet runner bean," said Mother. "Pretty flowers grow from them, and so we shall plant them in our flower garden."

Betty held some beans in her hand.

"Do we have to plant all of them?" she asked. "May I keep some?"

"You may keep the ones you have," said Mother. "We will plant the others. But we will keep them, too."

"Keep them!" said Betty. "Why, Mother, when you plant the seeds, they will be gone, won't they?"

Mother said, "Wait and see."

They planted the scarlet runner beans, and this is what happened to each one.

Water from the soil soaked into the seed. It soaked through the seed coat into the stored food. Then it carried some of the food into the root of the baby plant.

The food made the baby plant begin to grow.

First the little root grew down into the soil, and more roots branched out from it.

Look at the beans that you planted. Are there roots on them?

As the little root grew larger, it soaked up water from the soil. The water went into the tiny stem and leaves, and the food in the seed went with it.

So the leaves and stem began to grow. Up through the soil they went, into the sunlight!

Then the leaves opened out, and the plant began to make food.

Plants grew from all the scarlet runner seeds. As the days went by, their roots grew longer and thicker.

The stems grew higher and lifted the leaves farther and farther up into the warm sunlight.

The leaves grew larger, and many more leaves came out from the stems.

Then the plants were big and strong.

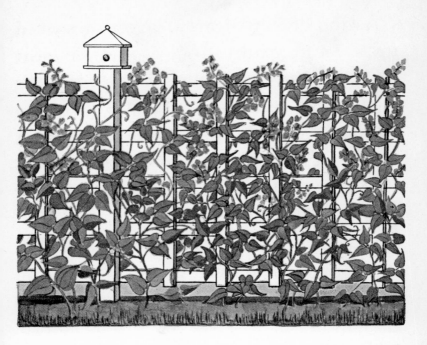

Tiny green buds grew on the plants. In a few days the buds had bloomed into pretty flowers with scarlet petals.

Betty wanted to pick the flowers, but her mother said, "Don't pick them all."

"Why not?" asked Betty.

"You will find out if you watch them for a few days," said Mother.

Betty watched the scarlet blossoms. In a few days she saw that something was happening to them.

 Inside the flowers small green pods were growing. The flower petals fell off, and the pods grew longer and longer.

When the pods were brown and dry, Betty's mother opened one of them.

"Look," she said. "Now do you see why the flowers had to stay on the plants?"

 "Oh!" cried Betty. "There are seeds in the pods! Did the flowers make them?"

"Yes," said Mother. "All seeds grow from flowers."

Betty said, "These seeds are just like the ones we planted. Now I see why we plant seeds to keep them."

DANDELION   TREE   WHEAT

Roots

Dandelions have one thick root, which grows straight down into the soil.

Trees have many roots. The roots are very large, and they branch out.

Roots of wheat plants look like strings.

Pull up some bean plants from your window box. What do the roots look like?

There are many kinds of roots, but all roots do the same thing for the plant.

They soak up water.

ROSE

CACTUS

CORN

Stems

Are all these stems alike?

Do they all have branches?

Is the stem of the rose as large as the stem of the cactus or the corn plant?

Stems may be big or little or long or short. But all stems do the same thing for the plant. They carry water from its roots to its leaves.

And the stems of most plants lift the leaves up into the light.

Leaves

Are the blades of the elm leaf and the nasturtium leaf shaped alike?

Do the veins grow the same way?

Are any of the leaves in the picture just alike?

Each kind of plant has leaves that are different from the leaves of other kinds of plants. But most leaves are green. And all green leaves do the same thing for the plant on which they grow.

They make its food.

87

WILD ROSE   SUNFLOWER   MAPLE

Flowers

Look at the picture and find the flowers that grow on maple trees.

Are maple flowers like the flowers that grow on peach trees or apple trees?

Are wild roses and sunflowers alike?

Do you know any two kinds of flowers that are just alike?

Many, many plants have flowers, and every kind of flower is different. But all flowers do the same thing.

They make seeds.

Seeds

Are all these seeds the same size?

How else are they different?

Seeds grow in many different ways.

Seeds of peanuts grow in pods. Peach and apple seeds grow inside the fruit.

Name some other kinds of seeds and tell how they grow.

There are many kinds of seeds.

But in every seed is a baby plant, with food that it uses when it begins to grow.

Parts of Plants

All the pictures on page 91 show parts of plants.

What parts of a plant do you see in Picture 1? What parts are in each of the other pictures?

Which pictures show:
1. the part that soaks up water from the soil?
2. the part where the plant's food is made?
3. the part that carries water from the roots to the leaves of the plant?
4. the part that holds the leaves up to the light?
5. the part from which seeds grow?
6. parts from which new plants grow?
7. parts where food is stored?

HOW LIVING THINGS HELP US

Food from Plants

Jim and Betty had gone with Mother to the store. While Mother was getting some meat for dinner, the children looked at the vegetables and fruit.

"There are peaches and oranges and apples," said Betty.

"And lettuce and carrots and beets and onions," said Jim. "My, there are many different kinds of fruit and vegetables!"

Mother came up and said, "Yes, there are many kinds. But they are all alike in one way. They are all parts of plants.

"A head of lettuce is the plant's leaves. The carrots and the beets are roots, and the potatoes and onion bulbs are stems."

"Apples and oranges and peaches all grow on plants, too," said Jim. "They are fruit, and they have the seeds of the plant inside them."

Mother looked at the vegetables.

"We need green vegetables for dinner," she said. "I'll take some peas and lettuce."

"Oh!" said Betty. "Peas are seeds, and so are beans and corn. They are parts of plants, too!"

"It's a good thing we have plants," said Jim. "If we didn't, we would not have anything to eat but meat."

"We would have milk," said Betty. "Milk comes from cows."

"Why, Jim and Betty!" said Mother. "How many cows do you think there would be if we didn't have any plants?"

Both children looked surprised.

"Cows must have food," said Mother.

"That's right," said Betty. "Cows eat grass and other kinds of plants. So if we didn't have any plants, we could not have any milk."

Jim said, "We could not have any meat, either. There would not be any pigs or sheep or chickens if they didn't have plants to eat."

"Is there any food that does not come from plants?" asked Betty.

"Look around the store," said Mother. "See if there is any food here that does not come from plants."

Jim and Betty looked and looked.

Suddenly Betty said, "Oh, Jim! This is a fine game! Maybe we can play it at school tomorrow.

"We can have the children try to think of foods that do not come from plants."

"Yes," said Jim. Then he laughed and said, "But it will not be an easy game.

"You and I looked all over the store, but we didn't find any kind of food that does not come from plants!"

Name some roots that we eat.
Name some stems that we eat.
Name some leaves that we eat.
Name some seeds that we eat.

Playing the Food Game

The children at school all wanted to play Betty and Jim's new game.

They all tried to think of some kind of food that does not come from a plant.

Tom was first. He said, "Eggs."

Miss Young said, "If Tom is right, he may have another turn.

"Who can tell us if Tom is right?"

"Eggs come from hens," said Patty. "Hens eat corn and wheat, and they are plants. So eggs really come from plants."

"That's right," said Miss Young. "Now it is Patty's turn."

Patty said, "Bread."

"Bread comes from wheat," said Joe. "And wheat is a plant."

It was Joe's turn, and he said, "Sugar."

Do you think he was right? Why?

Things to Find Out

Name the foods in the picture.

Where does milk come from?

Where does butter come from?

Where does sugar come from?

Find out how plants help make each of the other foods in the picture.

Can you think of any food that does not come from plants?

Clothing Makers

Look at the picture of Tom and Sally. Do you think their clothes are pretty?

Sally's clothes are made of cotton.

The cotton grew on cotton plants in the south.

This picture shows a cotton plant.

Cotton grows in a pod. When the pod opens, the cotton is picked. Then it is made into cloth.

Tom has on linen clothes. Linen is made from stems of plants like this.

Find out what kind of plant it is.

In winter Tom and Sally have warm clothing made from wool. Wool is the hair that grows on sheep. The wool is cut off the sheep and made into cloth.

Tom's and Sally's shoes came from an animal, too. Find out what part of an animal is used to make shoes.

All of Tom's and Sally's clothing come either from a plant or from an animal.

Look about you and name the kinds of clothing that you see. What animal or plant does each kind come from?

Do you see any clothes that do not come from animals or plants?

Animal and Plant Friends

Here is a picture of Tom and Sally and their pets.

Tom is tired and warm, and so he is sitting in the shade of the big trees.

Sally is picking some flowers to take into the house.

Look at the picture and tell how the trees have helped make a pretty yard.

What other plants have helped make the yard pretty?

Is the house made of wood?

Where does wood come from?

What things do we use in our homes that are made of wood?

What pets are in the picture?

What pets do you have? Why do you like to have pets?

What animals do we see on farms?

What farm animals are used for food?

Wool clothes come from sheep. Name another kind of clothes that come from farm animals.

What do farmers use their horses for?

Who else uses a horse to help him do his work?

Pests or Friends?

Farmers grow many plants on their farms. People and animals must have plants to use for food.

There are many, many insects that eat the plants. These insects are not friends of the farmer. They are pests.

Find an insect pest on page 56 and tell why it is a pest.

Animals that eat insect pests are friends of the farmer.

On page 57 find two animals that are friends of the farmer. Tell why they are his friends.

Is a garden spider a friend? Why?

Another animal friend often lives in gardens and eats insects. He goes hop, hop over the ground. When he was a baby, he lived in water. What is he?

Mice eat corn and wheat. Are mice pests or friends?

Find an animal friend on page 55 and tell why it is a friend.

Weeds are plants that we do not use. If weeds grow in fields and gardens, other plants do not have enough room to grow.

Are weeds pests or friends?

Some birds eat many, many weed seeds. So they help to keep new weeds from growing. Are they pests or friends?

Find a bird friend on page 58 and tell why he is a friend.

Look at the pictures of living things in your book. Write the names of the ones that are friends. Write the names of the ones that are pests.

When you are outdoors, look for living things. Find out which ones are friends and which ones are pests.

LAND + WATER

Going to the Ocean

THE TRIP TO THE CITY

Jim and Betty were going for a long, long trip. All the way to the ocean!

They were going in an airplane to see Grandmother, who lived in the west.

First, Mother and Father had to take them in the car as far as the big city. There the children would get into the airplane.

It took all day to go to the city. The road went through flat land, and the children could see far in every direction.

On each side of the road were flat, green fields where horses and cows and sheep were eating grass. There were fields of corn and wheat, too.

Sometimes the road went on a bridge across a small river or creek. Once two creeks came together near the road and made one large creek.

"Other creeks run into this one as it goes along," said Mother. "So the farther it goes, the larger it gets.

"A long way from here it runs into a big river. You will fly over the river in the airplane."

On and on went the car through fields and woods.

Suddenly Betty cried, "Oh, look! I see the ocean!"

Mother laughed. "Oh, no," she said. "That is only a big lake. It is one of the biggest lakes in the world. But the ocean is much larger than any lake."

THE AIRPLANE TRIP

That night Mother and Father and the children stayed in the city. Very early the next morning they all went in their car to the airplane field.

The big airplane was all ready to start. Mother and Father helped Betty and Jim into it. Then they said good-by.

Soon the airplane started. It rolled along the ground very fast. All at once it was off the ground and in the air.

What a noise it made! The children put cotton in their ears to shut out the noise.

Higher and higher they went.

Jim pointed down toward the ground.

Betty looked down and saw that the houses and people looked as small as toys.

Out over the flat land went the airplane. The children kept watching the ground, and after a while they saw a big river.

"That must be the big river Mother told us about!" cried Jim.

Across the river the land was not flat. There were low hills, and the roads and creeks went in and out around them.

Soon the land was flat again as far as the children could see. They were crossing the part of the land that is called plains. The roads were as straight as arrows, and there were not many rivers or trees.

The children grew tired of watching the flat plains and went to sleep. When they woke up, it was time for lunch.

"Will we ever come to the ocean?" Betty thought. She looked out of the window.

"Oh, look!" she cried, and pointed down.

Jim looked down and saw some big hills. Farther on there were high mountains. The tops of some of them were covered with snow.

"There are the mountains!" cried Jim. "We are going to cross them."

Between some of the mountains were low places called valleys. In the valleys were rivers, lakes, fields, and farmhouses.

After they crossed the mountains, they flew over a desert. This part of the land was very dry, for a desert does not have much rain.

There were no creeks or rivers, and the soil was dry dust and sand.

There were no trees, for trees cannot grow in so dry a place. But there were small cactus plants and some dry grass.

The airplane crossed the desert and more mountains. Then it flew over a big valley. But the children did not see the valley, for their eyes were shut.

They were fast asleep!

When they woke up, the airplane was on the ground. And there were Grandmother and Grandfather, laughing at Betty and Jim for being asleep.

The long airplane trip was over!

As the children walked to Grandfather's car, they kept looking all around.

"What are you looking for?" Grandfather asked them.

"The ocean," said Jim. "Where is it?"

"We thought we would see it as soon as we got here," said Betty.

"Why!" said Grandfather. "Didn't either of you see it from the airplane?"

"No," said Jim. "We were both asleep."

"Well, well!" laughed Grandfather.

"Hop into my car, and we will go out to the ocean right now!"

The car went along very fast.

Suddenly Grandfather said, "Look!"

And there, as far as they could see, was blue, blue water.

There was the ocean at last!

A Sand Picture

When Jim and Betty came home from the west, they told all their friends about their airplane trip.

They told about seeing the plains and the mountains and the desert.

The other children had never seen plains or mountains. They had not seen cactus or even heard of a desert.

"What is a desert?" they asked. "What is cactus?

"What do the mountains and the plains look like?"

Jim and Betty could not tell the other children just what the mountains and plains and desert looked like.

"But I think we can show you what they are like," said Jim. "We can make them in our sand-box."

Jim and Betty made the sand-box look like this picture.

They used blue paper to make a river. They pulled up grass and used it to show plains and green valleys.

What else did they show?

What is the land like near your home?

Can you make a sand picture of it?

Where Water Goes

Do rain and snow stay on the ground? When rain falls or when snow melts, some of the water soaks into the ground. But some of it runs along on top of the ground.

Water runs from high parts of the land to the low parts. It runs into creeks. Creeks run together and make rivers, and rivers run into the oceans.

Sometimes a river runs into a low valley and makes a lake.

Look at the picture on page 111.
Find a green valley.
Find a river in the valley.
What does the river run into?
Where is snow in the picture?
When the snow melts, where will the water go?

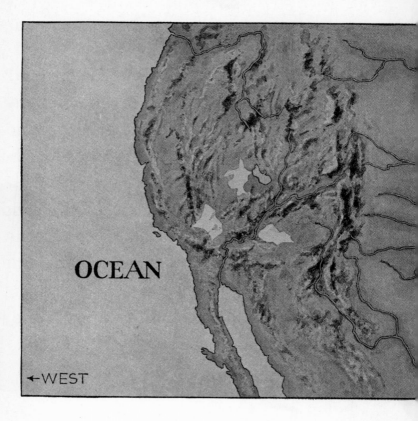

OCEAN

←WEST

Land and Water

The picture on these two pages shows land and water in part of America.

The green shows land that has rain.

The yellow shows deserts.

118

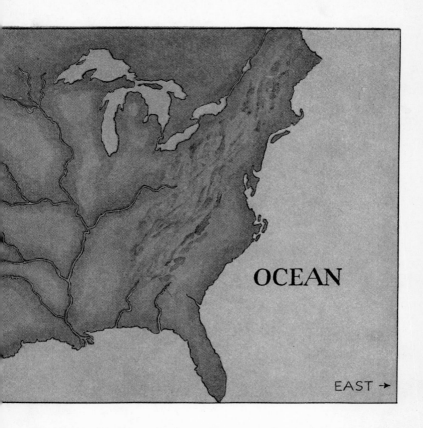

OCEAN

EAST →

The blue shows the parts that are water.
Find the ocean on the east.
Find the ocean on the west.
Find the parts that have mountains.
Find some lakes and rivers.

How Do We Use Land?

The food we eat grows on land. We build our houses and towns on land.

Where do we get wood to build houses? What else is wood used for?

What is stone used for? Where does stone come from?

Coal comes from the ground. Tell some other things we get from the ground.

How Do We Use Water?

Turn to the picture on page 15.

How is the water being used?

Plants use water from the soil to make their food. What do we use plants for?

What food comes from rivers and lakes and oceans?

Could animals live without water?

How do you use water?

Do You Know?

1. What are plains?

2. What do we call parts of the land where there is no water?

3. What kinds of plants grow in a desert?

4. Which are higher, mountains or hills?

5. What is a valley?

6. When snow melts, where does the water go?

7. Where does water go when it rains?

8. How are rivers made?

9. What do rivers run into?

10. How is a lake made?

11. What is west of America?

12. What is east of America?

13. Which is larger, an ocean or a lake?

14. Which is larger, a river or a creek?

15. Tell how we use water.

16. Tell how we use land.

SUN·MOON·STARS

THE SUN

How Big Is the Sun?

Dick and Jane sat looking at the red sun as it was going down. Dick said it looked as big as a dish-pan. Jane said it was the size of her new umbrella.

Father came out just then, and Jane asked how big the sun looked to him.

"Oh, about the size of a penny," he said. "I can hide it with a penny."

He shut one eye and held a penny in front of his open eye.

Jane and Dick did what Father did.

They could see no sun at all!

"Go to the corner of the yard and look at the house," said Father. "See if you can hide it with a penny."

Dick and Jane ran to the corner of the yard. They each shut one eye and held a penny in front of the other eye.

They could not see the house at all!

"Now walk up near the house and see if the penny hides it," said Father.

The children tried, but they could not hide the house when they were near it. It looked much larger than the penny.

Father said, "Big things look smaller when they are far away. The farther away they are, the smaller they look.

"The sun is a long, long way from us, and so it looks small. But it is really a great many times larger than the earth.

"The moon is smaller than the earth. But it is much nearer to us than the sun, and so it looks as large as the sun."

"Let's play that the sun is the size of my umbrella," said Jane. "What should we use to show how much smaller the moon is?"

"Use the head of a pin," said Father. "And use a pea for the earth."

"Oh!" cried Dick. "I thought the sun and the moon were the same size, but the sun is really much larger."

"It is much larger than the earth, too," said Jane. "The sun is the largest of all!"

How the Sun Helps Us Live

THE SUN HEATS THE EARTH

The sun looks like a great ball of fire, and is very, very hot. If it were near the earth, nothing could live on the earth. It would be too hot.

In summer the sun's heat makes us warm. In winter we build fires in stoves to keep our houses warm, and we put on thick clothes when we go outdoors.

But even in winter we get some heat from the sun. If we didn't, we could not live. Nothing in the world could live, for the earth would be too cold.

THE SUN LIGHTS THE EARTH

All our daylight comes from the sun. What happens when the sun goes down? What happens when it comes up?

All through the day we have light from the sun and can see the things about us.

Even on cloudy days light comes to us from the sun.

Cloudy days are darker than sunny days because the clouds come between the earth and the sun. They shut off some of the sun's light.

But the sun is shining on the other side of the clouds, and some of its light comes through them.

If sunlight did not come through clouds, a cloudy day would be as dark as night.

Look on page 76 and find another way that sunlight helps us.

THE SUN TELLS TIME

Long, long ago there were no clocks. People told time by the sun.

How could they tell when it was noon?

Sometimes people made shadow sticks like the one in the picture, and told time by them.

In the early morning, when the sun was low in the east, the stick made a very long shadow. As the sun climbed higher in the sky, the shadow got shorter. By noon there was almost no shadow at all.

In the afternoon, as the sun went lower in the west, the shadow grew longer.

People watched the shadow just as we watch our clocks. When the shadow was very short, it was time to have lunch.

In the afternoon, when the shadow was very long, it was time to stop work and go home.

Sun clocks were used long ago, too. A sun clock shows the hours as our clocks do. A shadow points to the hour as the hand of a clock does.

Look at the picture and tell what hour the sun clock shows.

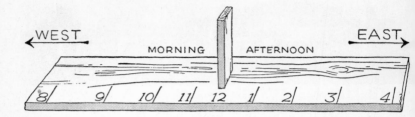

Making a Shadow Stick

You can make a shadow stick. Get a board and nail a short stick to it.

Put the board outdoors where the sun will shine on it all day. Put it on the ground, with the ends pointing east and west. The stick will make a shadow on the board.

Look at the board each hour and make a line on it where the shadow falls. On the line write what time it is.

What time does the shadow show:

1. when you come to school?
2. when you go home to lunch?
3. when you go home in the afternoon?

THE MOON

When Do We See the Moon?

The moon does not come up at the same time each night. It comes up about an hour later every night. At last it comes up so late that it is in the sky in the daytime!

Have you ever seen the moon in the daytime? What did it look like?

Can you tell why the moon does not look bright in the daytime?

Sometimes clouds cover the moon at night. Then the earth is very dark. Tell why clouds make the earth darker.

There are a few nights in each month when we cannot see the moon at all. Then the moon is new.

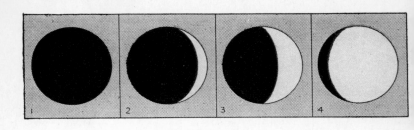

How the Moon Tells Time

How do we know when a week has gone by?

How many weeks are in a month?

The pictures show how the moon can tell us when a month has gone by.

The moon is new once each month.

At first when the moon is new, we do not see it. But a few nights later we see a small part of it.

When we first see the new moon, it looks like the yellow part of Picture 2.

Each night we see a larger part of the moon. In about two weeks the moon looks like Picture 5. Then it is a full moon.

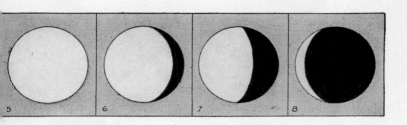

After the moon is full, we say it is an old moon. A smaller part of it shows each night until two weeks have gone by. Then the moon looks like the yellow part of Picture 8.

A few nights later it cannot be seen at all, and the new moon begins again.

From one new moon to the next new moon is about a month. Long ago people watched the moon to tell when a month had gone by.

What kind of moon will there be tonight?
How will it change?
Find out how long it will be before you can see the same kind of moon again.

Does the Moon Give Light?

The boy in the picture is catching the sunlight in a looking glass. He makes the sunlight shine on the wall or anywhere he wants it to.

The moon is like a looking glass. It has no light of its own. But it catches the sun's light and makes it shine back on the earth.

We say this light is moonlight. But it really is sunlight.

THE STARS

Star Stories

Joe and Patty were watching for the first star to come out.

When it came out, they both looked at it and said,

"Star light, star bright,
First star I see tonight;
I wish I may, I wish I might
Have the wish I wish tonight."

Then they each made a wish.

Joe laughed and said, "The first star can't really give us our wishes, but it's fun to think it can."

"What makes that one star come out before the others do?" asked Patty.

"The others are really in the sky now," said Joe. "They are always in the sky, but we cannot see them when the sunlight is bright. This star is brighter than the others, and so we can see it sooner.

"In a little while we can see the Big Dipper and a great many other stars."

"I know a Dipper story," said Patty.

"Once a little girl carried some water to her mother in a dipper. After the girl had given the water to her mother the dipper suddenly changed to stars and went up into the sky."

"That's a good story," said Joe. "Once I read a story about the stars. The story said that long ago all the stars were in a large jar. A man was putting the stars up in the sky to make star pictures.

"He had just put up the Big Dipper when a coyote came along.

"The man told the coyote not to touch the jar of stars. But the coyote pushed the cover off the jar, and all the stars went up into the sky. So the man could not make any more star pictures."

"That's a good story, too," said Patty. "But did you know that some people say the Dipper looks like a wagon? They say the wagon is pulled by three horses."

"It's dark enough to see the Dipper now," cried Joe. "The four stars in the bowl of the Dipper are the wagon. The three stars in the handle are the horses."

The North Star

We can tell directions by one star in the sky. It is called the North Star.

It is always in the north. When you are looking at it, you are looking north.

It is easy to find the North Star in the sky if you first find the Big Dipper. Two of the stars in the bowl of the Dipper point straight to the North Star. They are numbered 1 and 2 in the picture.

Sometimes the Dipper is on one side of the North Star, and sometimes on the other side. But the bowl of the Dipper is always turned toward it, and the two stars always point straight at it.

The Milky Way

If you look at the sky some dark night, you will see the Milky Way. It is like a bright road across the sky.

Some people call it "The Little White Sister of the Rainbow." And others call it a river with little bright fish in it.

The Milky Way is really a great many stars that are near together. They are so far away from us that we cannot see them. We only see some of the light that comes from them. The light from all of these stars together is the Milky Way.

MAKING WORK EASY

MACHINES

How the Stone Was Moved

Dick was helping Jane make her garden.

He was digging up the black earth with his spade.

"Let's take out that stone," said Jane. "Then there will be more room for my vegetables."

"That is a big stone," said Dick. "But I think we can move it."

He and Jane pulled and pushed. They could not move the stone.

Jane asked Father to help them. But he could not move the stone, either.

He said, "Part of the stone goes down into the ground. We can't lift it out with our hands. We must use a lever."

"What is a lever?" asked the children.

"I'll show you," answered Father.

"Dick, please get me a brick from the big flower bed."

Father pushed the sharp end of the spade under the stone as far as it would go. Then he put the brick on the ground under the spade.

"Now, Dick," he said, "push down on the handle of the spade."

Dick pushed down on the end of the handle, and the other end of the spade pushed up on the stone.

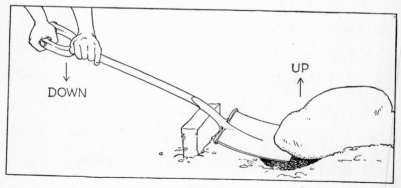

142

Father said, "The spade and the brick are a lever. They help lift the stone."

As Dick pushed down on the lever, it slowly lifted the stone out of the ground.

"Now I can roll the stone out of the garden," said Dick.

He rolled it a little way and stopped. "My!" said Dick. "This is hard work!"

Father said, "I know an easier way to move the stone out of the garden. Run and get your wagon, Dick."

Dick got his wagon, and Father lifted the stone into it.

Dick began to pull the wagon.

The wagon wheels began to turn. They rolled along the ground.

"Oh!" said Dick in great surprise. "The stone is not heavy now!"

His father said, "It is just as heavy as it was before. But the wheels on the wagon make it easier to move."

Dick said, "The lever helped, too. It lifted the stone out of the ground."

"Yes," said Father. "Levers and wheels are good helpers."

Wheels

Get four large books and tie them together with a piece of string. Tie the end of the string to your little finger.

Try to pull the books across the table with your finger. Is it easy?

Now put the books in a toy wagon and see if you can pull them with your little finger. Which way is easier? Do wheels make it easy to pull heavy things?

Which of these pictures shows a way to make work easier?

Levers

Tie the string around your little finger again.

Now try to lift the books that you put in the wagon.

Is it easy to lift them with your finger?

Put the books on a table. Make a lever with a stick and a small piece of wood.

Put one end of the lever under the books. Push down on the other end with your little finger.

Does the lever make it easy to lift the books with your little finger?

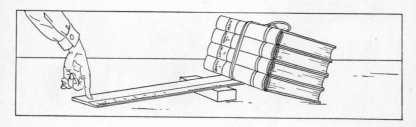

Can you pull a nail out of a piece of wood with your fingers? Try it and see.

Now try to pull the nail out with a hammer. Put the claws of the hammer under the nail and pull down on the handle.

Does the nail come out?

When you use a hammer to pull out a nail, you are using a lever.

The claws of the hammer are one end of the lever, and the handle is the other end. You pull down on the handle and make the claws push up on the head of the nail. So the nail is lifted out.

Have you ever tried to lift something that was too heavy for you?

Could you have lifted it with a lever?

Name some heavy things that might be lifted with a lever.

How Machines Help Us

Machines are helpers. We use them to make our work easier. Levers and wheels are machines. There are many machines that we use every day. On the next page are pictures of some of them.

Which picture shows a machine for cutting paper and cloth?

Which one is used to roll out dough?

Find two machines that are used to cut wood.

Which machine is used for digging?

Name the other machines on the page and tell what work each one helps to do.

What machines are used to do work in your home?

What other machines have you seen people using?

Tell what kind of work they do.

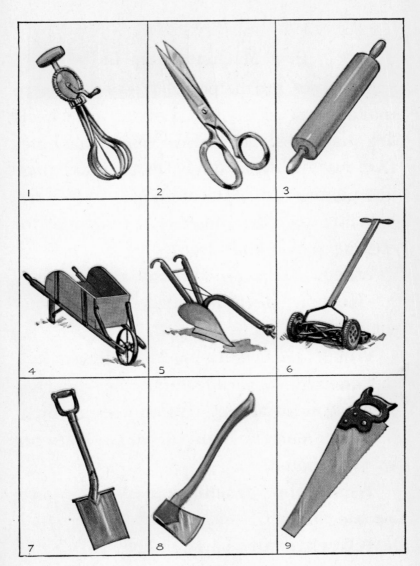

149

ELECTRICITY

Using Electricity

One day Nancy and Father and Mother made a trip to the city. While they were away, there was a thunder storm. It was very dark when they got home.

Father opened the front door and went in. He pushed the electric light button, but no lights came on.

"Well!" said Mother. "Something has happened to the lights."

Father went through the house pushing the other electric light buttons. But no lights came on.

"The lightning has done something to our electricity," said Father. "We shall have to go to bed in the dark."

"There is a candle on the table by the south window," said Mother.

Nancy and Mother could hear Father walk across the room. They heard him strike a match. They saw the match blaze as it moved up to the candle.

"Now we can see," said Father. "We must hurry to bed, for this candle will not last long."

He held the candle high, so that Mother and Nancy could see their way.

The next day was bright and sunny. They did not need electric lights. But they did need electricity.

Nancy's mother could not use her new electric stove. She had to make a fire with coal in the old stove.

She could not use her electric washing machine.

She could not use her electric sweeper, and so it took her a long time to sweep the floors.

She was very hot and tired when she was through her work that day.

In the evening, just as it was beginning to get dark, the house suddenly blazed with light.

They had electricity again!

"Candle-light is pretty," said Nancy. "But electric lights are brighter. And now we can use our electric helpers."

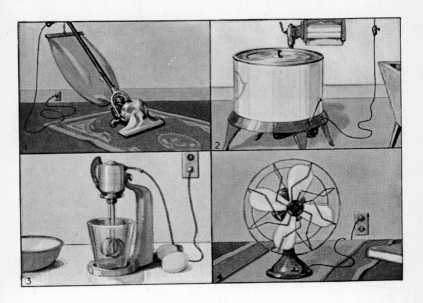

Electric Helpers

Electricity is one of our best helpers. Electric lights make our rooms brighter than candles do. Electricity runs many machines that do work for us.

Name the electric machines in the picture and tell what work they do.

Name some other electric machines, and tell how they help us.

The Fire Helper

Fire is one of our helpers.

It keeps our homes warm in winter.

How does fire help get our food ready for us to eat?

Have you ever watched a fire burning old leaves or papers? It helps us when it burns these things.

How did fire help Nancy and her mother and father, when something happened to their electric lights?

Fire can help us in many ways if we know how to take care of it. But before we can use fire, we have to know:

How to make a fire.

How to put out a fire.

How to Make a Fire

Ann lived on a farm and took her lunch to school. She often took gingerbread cookies in her lunch. They were shaped like fat little men. They had black eyes, and black buttons down their fronts.

Sometimes Ann took some cookies to her friends at school.

M-m-m-m, how good the cookies were!

One morning Ann said to Miss Field, "Mother wants everyone to come home with me and bake gingerbread men."

So that afternoon Miss Field and the children went to Ann's house.

Ann's mother took them to her kitchen. On a table were some big bowls. There were sugar and butter and milk and all the things for gingerbread. And there were cookie cutters like fat little men!

"First we must build a fire in the stove and heat the oven," said Ann's mother.

In a corner of the kitchen was a big black stove. Near it were some sticks of wood and some paper and coal. And on a table were some matches.

Ann's mother took the covers off the stove and showed the children where the fire should be made.

"Who knows how to make a fire?" asked Miss Field.

"First the paper goes in," said Billy.

"All right, Billy," said Miss Field. "You may put it in. Now what goes in next?"

"Wood," said Bob. He went to the box and picked up a big, thick piece of wood.

"That is not right," said Billy. "Some small pieces of wood should go in before the big ones. Small pieces will catch fire more quickly."

So Bob picked out some small pieces of wood and put them on top of the paper.

"Now put the big pieces in," said Billy.

When the big pieces of wood were in, Miss Field put in some coal.

"Now everything is ready," she said. "If we heat the paper very hot, it will burn and start our fire.

"We shall heat it with a match."

Miss Field lighted a match and held the blaze to the paper. The blaze heated the paper and made it catch fire.

Then Miss Field put the covers back on the stove.

The paper blazed up quickly and heated the small pieces of wood.

So the small pieces caught fire and heated the larger pieces of wood, until they began to blaze.

Hotter and hotter grew the coal, until at last it was so hot that it caught fire and began to burn, too.

"Now we must put in more coal," said Ann's mother. "Coal burns more slowly than wood, and so a coal fire lasts longer than a wood fire."

After the coal was in, smoke began to come out of the stove into the kitchen.

The fire almost stopped blazing.

"Oh, the fire is going out!" cried Ann.

Her mother said, "The fire is not getting enough air.

"Open the little door on the front of the stove to let in more air."

Ann opened the door, and the stove stopped smoking at once.

"Hear the fire cracking!" she said. "It has started to blaze again.

"Soon it will make the oven hot enough to bake our gingerbread men."

While the oven was getting hot, they made the gingerbread men.

Butter, sugar, flour, and all the things for gingerbread dough were put into the bowls and made into soft dough.

Soon the dough was on the table, and the children rolled it flat.

Cut, cut, cut, went the cookie cutters.

In went the black eyes, and in went the buttons, and there on the table were the gingerbread men!

Into the oven they went, and were baked a beautiful brown.

Then home went the happy children, with the gingerbread men that their fire had baked.

Things to Find Out

Here are some things to find out about fire. But your teacher must help you, or you might burn your hands.

Some things will burn.

Some things will not burn.

Ask your teacher to help you find out if these things will burn:

| sand | glass | water |
| bricks | stones | earth |

Ask your teacher to help you find out which of these things catch fire quickly:

dry twigs	small stick of wood
coal	cotton cloth
wool cloth	cardboard
dry leaves	large stick of wood

Which would you use to start a fire?

Find out if wet things catch fire as quickly as dry things.

Will a fire burn without air? Here is a way to find out. But your teacher must help you.

Stand a candle in the sand on your sand-table and light it.

Turn a glass jar over it, so that no air can get under the jar. Watch and see what happens.

Light the candle again. Hold the jar up over it so that air can get under the jar.

Does the candle burn longer than it did the first time? Can you tell why?

Light a candle. Push the lighted end into the sand so that no air can get to the blaze. What happens?

Find out if water keeps air away from fire. Push the lighted end of a candle down into a jar of water. What happens?

How to Put Out a Fire

Fire often starts in places where we do not need it. Then it is not a helper.

Everyone should know how to put out fire, for it can burn us, and it can burn our homes.

What are the firemen in the picture using to put out the fire?

Why are the firemen putting water on the house that is not burning?

The boy is putting sand on a fire.

Have your teacher help you find out if that is a good way to put out fire.

Put some paper on your sand-table and light it. Then cover it with sand.

Push the sand away from the paper.

Has the blaze gone out? Why?

Light another paper and find out if water will put out the blaze. Would it be easy to light the paper again? Why?

Water puts out fire by keeping air away from it. And the water cools whatever is burning. Then it will not blaze again.

Do You Know?

1. What work can a lever help us do?

2. How do you use a lever to make it lift something?

3. What work do wheels make easy?

4. Name some machines that are run by electricity and tell what work they do.

5. Name two machines that are used to sweep floors.

6. Name three other machines used in your home. Tell what work they do.

7. Name three machines that a farmer uses. Tell what work they do.

8. Tell about some other work that is done by machines.

9. How does fire help us?

10. Name five things that will burn.

11. What does fire need to make it burn?

12. Tell two good ways to put out fire.

Tell the Answers

1. What makes rain?
2. What kinds of weather do we have?
3. What makes the weather warm?
4. How does wind change the weather?
5. How does rain change the weather?
6. Name some animals that hunt for their food. Tell how each one gets its food and what parts of its body it uses.
7. What animal makes a web? How does the web help it get food?
8. How do animals get food in winter?
9. How do plants get food?
10. Name the parts of a plant. Tell what each part does for the plant.
11. How do plants and animals help us?
12. Name three animals that are friends and three animals that are pests.
13. What kind of plants are pests?

14. How are the plains different from the mountains?

15. How are deserts and plains different?

16. When it rains, or when snow melts, where does the water go?

17. How does the sun help us live?

18. Where does moonlight come from?

19. How does the moon tell time?

20. How can you find the North Star?

21. What is the Milky Way?

22. Tell two ways in which electricity helps us.

23. What kind of work does a lever make easier?

24. What kind of work does a wheel make easier?

25. Name two things that will burn and two things that will not burn.

26. Tell how to make a fire.

27. Tell two ways to put out a fire.

TEACHER'S NOTES

This book is to be used as a textbook, so that definite assignments can be made throughout the school year. The teacher should acquaint herself with the underlying purpose of each unit and the suggestions for teaching. Survey the experiments and activities called for in the text, and plan for the time and materials required to work them out. (See paragraph 7, and notes for pp. 17, 25, 31, 32, 72, 73, 77-79). Particularly, plan the work so that the experiments on pp. 32, 72, and 73 will be properly timed. Detailed directions and other suggestions will be found in the teacher's manual.

Remember that the purpose of this book is to arouse the child's interest in his own immediate surroundings and guide him in understanding them. Pages where it is imperative to have local conditions well in mind and adapt discussions to them are listed: 12, 14, 15, 17, 25, 27, 28, 31, 38, 39, 40, 48-50, 54-64, 83-89, 95, 99, 101, 102, 103, 116, 117, 120, 126-127, 148, 154.

At all times encourage an attitude of respect for scientific procedure. Insist on accuracy in observation and the following of directions; avoid drawing hasty conclusions; experiment to solve a definite problem that is clearly before the class.

Note that for Parts One and Two an introductory story (pp. 7, 43) gives a preview of the unit and introduces its principal ideas.

Materials needed for experiments and activities required by text:

Page 16. For each child, a square of colored paper; a strong pin; a short length of lath.

Page 25. Large cardboards for chart; crayons; small squares of blue, gray, and white paper, small cutouts of umbrella; pinwheel (p. 16); wind vane (see teacher's manual for directions for making).

Page 31. Room thermometer; outdoor thermometer.

Page 32. Teakettle (not teapot); stove or electric plate; pan or plate and a means of cooling it.

Page 72. Experiment 1: Young growing plants; water glass or bottle; red ink. Experiment 2: Grass seed; two flower pots filled with garden loam; a place where they can be put in total darkness.

Page 73. Potato experiment: a firm, well-matured potato; two hat pins; a water glass. Experiment 1: Beans; window-box. Experiment 2: Beans; glass or jar with clear sides.

Page 79. Beans.

Page 85. Bean plants.

Page 116. Sand table; grass, colored paper, and other materials to model a scene of local land formations and bodies of water.

Page 145. Four large books; a piece of strong string; a toy wagon with wheels that turn easily.

Page 146. Same books as 145; stick or heavy ruler; block of wood.

Page 147. Hammer; nail; block of wood.

Page 161. All articles listed on page; matches.

Page 162. Candle; matches; jar; water; sand.

Page 164. Paper; matches; sand; water.

Underlying Purpose of Part I, Weather: (1) To observe different kinds of weather in all seasons; (2) To observe the influence of weather on human activites; (3) To lay a foundation for understanding the cause and effect relationships between wind, moisture, and temperature that bring about weather changes.

Page 16: Pinwheel. See materials needed, p. 168.

Pages 17-31. Daily observation of force, direction, and temperature of the wind should be made, to draw conclusions of their effect on weather. (See weather-chart activities, pp. 24, 25, 31.)

Page 23: The Wind Vane. Be sure that the terminology (taught on page 19) is understood here and used. (See directions in the teacher's manual for making a wind vane.)

Pages 25, 31: The Weather Chart. See p. 168 for materials needed. Leave space for a temperature column (p. 31).

Provide a thermometer for class use. Take the temperature three times each day outdoors *in the shade* and record the temperature on the weather chart. Exercise 3 on page 31 directs the child in analyzing the factors (clouds, amount of sunshine, wind force, and wind direction) which affected the temperature of the warmest days. For example, the chart may show that the warmest day had bright sunshine, a warm wind, or no wind. (The effect of humidity on temperature is not introduced at this level.) If a chart is kept by months, use this exercise at the end of each month.

Page 32, 37: Experiment. See p. 168 for materials needed. The water should be boiling by the time the pupils are ready to read p. 37.

Underlying Purpose of Part II, Living Things: To develop the understandings that (1) food is necessary for growth; (2) different animals have different food-getting structures and methods; (3) plants make

169

their food; (4) living things grow up to resemble the parent; (5) man is dependent on other living things.

Chapter I: How Animals Get Food. The exercise on page 48 acquaints the teacher with the children's knowledge and past experiences concerning the main ideas of the unit.

If possible have live animals brought into the classroom for observation. Stress the fact that wild animals must hunt and catch their food. Supplement by (1) discussions of the text pictures and pictures of other animals that furnish examples of similar and different methods of getting food; (2) trips to zoos, museums, farms, woods, etc.; (3) live specimens. Knowledge of what animals eat is necessary as a background to the understanding of food-getting habits and structures. For example, compare the flicker's food and the quail's; then contrast the flicker's long slender bill with the short thick bill of the seed eater.

Children should become interested in observing and conserving winter birds. If possible, a feeding table should be constructed near the school. Discuss the kinds of food needed, such as suet, grain, etc.

Page 58. Note the strong bill and claws and big feet of the owl and compare with the hawk, eagle, etc.

Page 59: Identification. This page reviews the technique set up in *Book One* and stimulates interest in observation and identification. Extend to the pictures on pp. 68, 69. Use similar technique for identifying other animals. Keep in mind that birds (quail, bluejays, etc.) vary in coloring in different localities.

Pages 60-61: Reproduction. The main point of these two pages is that each young animal must learn to get its own food as it grows and that its food is eventually the same as the parent animal's. But if it is desired, a side study of reproduction can be made here. Review facts taught in *Book One*. Stress the concept that animals grow up and reproduce their own kind. Mammal birth may be compared to egg-hatching if animals such as guinea pigs or rabbits, and fish, frogs, birds, etc., are observed in the classroom.

Chapter II. How Plants Get Food. It is not the purpose of this chapter to explain the complicated process of photosynthesis. The points to be stressed are: (1) Plants make their own food; (2) roots, stems, and leaves have definite functions in food making; (3) plants cannot make food without sunlight.

Pages 72-75: Experiment 1. See p. 168 for list of materials. Cut through the stems of the plant to show more clearly that the water

170

with the red coloring has gone up into them. (A stalk of celery may be put in red ink and used as an additional exhibit.) Try the experiment yourself before having the class try it, to gauge the time needed.

Page 73: Experiments. See p. 168 for materials needed. To function properly, the experiments must have time to develop before pp. 76 and 77 are read. Gauge the time needed by working them yourself before the class tries them.

Use several pieces of healthy, well-matured potato. It may be possible to secure one in which the eyes are already giving indication of sprouting. Cut it so that the most likely looking eyes will come close to the water when the potato is suspended as shown in the picture. Roots will grow from the eye as well as sprouts, and it is necessary for them to reach water quickly for speedy growth of the top. Halve the potato or quarter it; do not cut slices. Arrange several specimens to insure success. Keep enough water in the glasses so that the potatoes will touch water. Halve one potato, place it cut side down on a saucer or plate, and keep it moist. Additional experiments can be carried out along the same lines, to show the same principle, with flower bulbs, onion bulbs, carrots, parsnips, and turnips (using the top part of the root of the last three in saucers of water).

Plant enough beans and grass seeds to be sure of enough specimens. (See note for p. 79.) For the beans secure some scarlet runners if possible, and limas, navy beans, and other common varieties. The bean seeds will sprout sooner if they are soaked a day before planting. Note the differences in growth in the different varieties—for instance, the navy bean lifts its cotyledons (two halves of the seed, where the food is stored) above the ground, while the scarlet runner does not. Point out how these two "storehouses" of food change as the plant develops.

Children should conclude that their yellowish plants grown in the dark cannot make food, because they are not green. The question of how they can grow without food is answered on pp. 77, 78, and 79.

By observing that the yellowish plants turn green after several hours of sunlight and continue to grow, while those put back in the dark turn yellow again and die, the child will conclude that sunlight is necessary for food making.

Pages 77-79: Food Storage and Reproduction. The potato experiment (p. 73) should now be at the stage where the sprouted stems of new growth are at least an inch long. Place the potatoes in sunlight and observe the change of color and development of leaves. Compare with the picture on p. 77. Plant the sprouted potatoes in soil. Later, dig them up and compare the root growth with the picture on p. 77. Refer to the picture of a mature potato plant on p. 78 for a better understanding of the last paragraph on p. 77. If possible, the children should pull up matured potato plants for observation.

If the beans required on p. 79 are soaked overnight, they will be easier to split open. It would be interesting at this point, and for p. 81, to have beans sprouted and at several stages of development. Enough could be planted at the time p. 73 (see note) is worked out; or additional beans could be planted in sand or dropped on moist cotton a few days before the reading of these pages.

Underground stems may be a difficult concept. Supplement the text to show the differences between underground storage stems (bulbs are also an example) and storage roots.

Review seasonal adaptation in *Science Stories, Book One.*

Chapter III—How Living Things Help Us. Develop the idea of man's dependence on plant and animal life. Take the class to a food market for identification of different foods. Provide stalks of wheat, oats, corn, etc., and make a trip to a flour mill. Provide manufacturers' samples of raw cotton, flax, leather, rubber, etc.

Page 97. Common table salt and water are classed as foods. If these are mentioned, make clear that man could not exist on them.

Underlying Purpose of Part III, Land and Water; Pages 104-121: To teach (1) the earth's surface is composed of varying forms of land and water; (2) the water areas are replenished by precipitation; (3) water runs down hill; (4) physical environment affects our lives.

Pages 105-114. The text and pictures develop (1) above. The pictures are photographs taken on an airline from Chicago to the Pacific coast. (Betty and Jim live in the central part of Wisconsin.) Supplement the story as local needs indicate. Provide pictures which show topography from Chicago to the Atlantic Ocean. The terms *desert, mountain, plain, valley, river, lake,* and *creek* should be supplemented by local terms such as *mesa* or *prairie.*

Page 115: The Sand-Table. The children may model features of their physical environment in the sand. Arrange excursions to observe local land formations and to note how small streams empty into other bodies of water. Sand-table reproductions may aid in understanding the generic terms and the fact that water runs down hill.

Pages 118-119: Introduce map reading. Teach that /
map is north. The names of the oceans are not necess
them if desirable. On the map locate Chicago, San I.
the home of Betty and Jim. Model this map in the sand ʋ
large relief map from salt, flour, and water. (See directions in ma

Underlying Purpose of Part IV, Sun, Moon, and Stars; Pages 122-139: (1) To begin the development of an understanding of the relationships between the earth and other bodies of the universe; (2) to encourage interest in observation of heavenly bodies.

Pages 123-125. The shape of the earth, sun, and moon are not referred to in the story, as the concept that they are spheres cannot be made clear in a text at this level.

Pages 126-127. Review the seasonal temperature changes due to sunshine (*Book One*). The weather record activity affords further understanding that we get heat from the sun in winter. Refer to the picture on p. 27 to show effects of the sun's heat in winter.

The questions on p. 126 are designed to bring out that it grows dark when the sun goes down, and grows light when it comes up.

Pages 132-133: The Phases of the Moon. Stress the fact that the moon is invisible for a few days when it is first new. If possible, have a calendar that indicates the moon phases and teach the children to interpret it. (Later books of the series will develop the cause of the apparent change in the moon's shape.)

Underlying Purpose of Part V, Making Work Easy: To promote understanding of man's use of machines, electricity, and fire.

Page 141: Levers. It is not necessary to explain the principle of levers other than a first-class lever.

Pages 145, 146, 147: Experiments. See p. 168 for materials needed.

Pages 148-149. Add other examples to these illustrations of common machines. In many of them the wheel and axle or the lever will function. It is not necessary that the children recognize all of these; but in a few good examples, such as the steam shovel, tack puller, see-saw, and wheelbarrow, they should be able to recognize the principles of the lever and the wheel and axle.

Pages 161, 162, 164: Experiments. See p. 168 for materials needed. See that the experiments are performed under the safest possible conditions. Knowledge of combustible materials forms the basis for the understanding of how to put out fire and how to prevent destructive fires. Correlate this chapter with the safety program.

VOCABULARY

The following word list presupposes familiarity with the vocabulary of the *Basic Primer, Book One,* and *Science Stories, Book One. Science Stories, Book Two,* introduces 197 additional words of which 89 words (marked with asterisks) appear in *Basic, Book Two.*

8
clothes
*quickly

9
*cool
*dust
storm

10
lightning
thunder

11
games
*through

12
*often

13
*slowly
feel
breeze

14
papers
*else

15
windmills
wheel
pump

16
square
*piece
*corners

19
*second

20
*secret
*wall

21
*reading
*suddenly
vane

23
arrow
pointing

24
Monday
Tuesday
Wednesday
chart

25
*few

26
heat
shade
*between

27
*horses
melted

28
*touches

29
thermometer
temperature

30
line
*tops

31
*need
write

32
teakettle
stove

34
*rivers
*learned
spout
*small

35
vapor

36
float

37
*held
*near
*hand
*burn

38
*together
*heavy

39
fog
*smoke
*really

40
hail
*sleet

43
chipmunk
*paws
*cracked
*teeth

44
either
insects

45
*didn't
*quietly

46
fur
*feet
*larger

47
*mice
*young

48
*pets
*sharp
*both

49
*easy
neck
*pick

50
lifts
*fruit
*claws
body

51
Nanook
seals
jaws

52
walrus
tusks
strike

174

54
coyote
raccoon
pads
55
*hold
*pull
56
*spider
*hunt
*web
57
swallow
flicker
58
Bob-white
60
*even
61
*enough
62
skunk
64
deer
*great
65
bloomed
*farther
66
popper
68
*chickadees
69
*woodpecker
straight
71
lettuce
carrot
72
different
*teacher
soil

73
potato
*sides
75
*most
soaks
76
*world
78
beets
bulbs
onion
80
*high
scarlet
81
*happened
84
pods
86
cactus
88
peach
89
size
92
*meat
vegetables
oranges
94
*sheep
96
sugar
97
*butter
98
clothing
cotton
99
linen
wool

100
*friends
102
pests
105
ocean
city
*flat
106
creek
109
low
110
crossing
plains
111
mountains
valleys
112
desert
118
America
120
*build
*stone
coal
127
*ago
clocks
128
*shadow
*sticks
129
*hour
130
*board
nail
end
131
*later
month

135
stories
*might
136
*jar
137
*bowl
handle
139
Milky
141
machine
*spade
lever
142
*brick
143
easier
145
*tie
finger
147
*hammer
dough
150
electricity
electric
button
151
*candle
match
blaze
152
sweeper
155
*gingerbread
*men
*bake

INDEX OF SCIENCE CONTENT